PELE

The King of Soccer

Susan Canizares • Samantha Berger

Scholastic Inc.
New York • Toronto • London • Auckland • Sydney

Acknowledgments

Literacy Specialist: Linda Cornwell

Social Studies Consultant: Barbara Schubert, Ph.D.

Design: Silver Editions

Photo Research: Silver Editions

Endnotes: Elizabeth Scholl

Endnote Illustrations: Anthony Carnabucia

Photographs: Cover: Al Schwartz/Gamma Liaison; pp. 1–3, 7, 9: UPI/Corbis-Bettmann; pp. 4, 5, 8, 10–12: AP/Wide World Photos; p. 6: Al Schwartz/Gamma Liaison.

Library of Congress Cataloging-in-Publication Data
Canizares, Susan, 1960-
Pelé, the king of soccer / Susan Canizares, Samantha Berger.
p. cm. -- (Social studies emergent readers)
Summary: Simple text and photographs present the accomplishments of Pelé, who has been called the king of soccer.
ISBN 0-439-04577-0 (pbk.: alk. paper)
1. Pelé, 1940- --Juvenile literature. 2. Soccer players--
Brazil--Biography--Juvenile literature. [1. Pelé, 1940- .
2. Soccer players.] I. Berger, Samantha. II. Title. III. Series.
GV942.7.P42C35 1999

796.334'092--dc21
[B]

98-50493
CIP AC

8   9   10   08   03

Pele was a great soccer player.

He ran.

He kicked.

He jumped.

He flipped.

He scored,

and he won!

People watched.

People listened.

People cheered,

and people loved him.

Pele is called the king of soccer.

PELE

The King of Soccer

In a small village in Brazil called Tres Coracoes, which means "Three Hearts," Pele was born on October 23, 1940. He was named Edson Arantes do Nascimento by his parents.

Edson's father, Dondinho, was a professional soccer player, but he did not make much money. He taught Edson, who was nicknamed Dico at the time, how to play soccer as soon as he was old enough to walk. Dico did not own a soccer ball, so he learned to kick a ball his father had made for him out of rags tied together. He and the other village boys played in the street, in their bare feet.

By the time he was eight years old, Dico was recognized by his friends as the best soccer player in the village. They gave him the name "Pele," which means "The Black Pearl." It was not long before others noticed how good a player Pele was. When Pele was just 15, a retired professional soccer player named Waldemar de Brito believed Pele was good enough to try out for a professional team. It took Pele three attempts, but he was finally accepted to play for the Santos Soccer Club, the number-one team in Brazil at the time.

Just two years later, Pele was chosen to play on the team that Brazil sent to the 1958 World Cup Championship. The World Cup tournament is the biggest sporting event in the world. Teams from all the countries that play soccer participate, and the winning team is considered the best soccer team in the world. At age 17, Pele became a star and led the Brazilian team to win the World Cup.

Four years later, at the World Cup tournament in 1962, Pele and his team won the cup for Brazil again. Pele led his country to its third World Cup in 1970.

Pele had become the most famous soccer player in the world. Other countries very much wanted Pele to play for them, and some tried to hire him, offering Pele as much as $1 million. But the president of Brazil told them that Pele was part of Brazil's national treasure. That meant he would always play for Brazil.

Pele was so popular that in the middle of a war between two countries in Africa, both sides agreed to stop fighting for a day so he could travel through and play in a soccer game. When the game was over, there was another cease-fire for a day in order for Pele to travel back again. The armies from the two countries led Pele across the border between Nigeria and Biafra.

In 1974, just a few weeks before he turned 34, Pele played his last game for the Santos team. After years of being a world star and devoting most of his life to the game of soccer, Pele felt he wanted to spend more time with his wife and two young children. At the end of his final game for Brazil, a crowd of 120,000 yelled "Stay!" to Pele as he left the field.

Although soccer is the world's most popular game, it has not been one of our country's most popular sports. The first professional teams were formed in the U.S. in 1972, but not too many people attended the games. One team manager, Clive Toye of the New York Cosmos, thought that if there was a star in American soccer, the game would become more popular. He decided to ask Pele to come to the U.S. and help soccer to become a serious professional sport here.

Pele accepted the offer and signed a $4 million contract. Toye's idea was a good one. With Pele on the team, people lined up to buy tickets for the Cosmos games. Pele appeared on television, and there were many newspaper articles about him. When people saw Pele on TV or read about him, they learned more about soccer. Pele said, "I came to your country because my dream is to help soccer here."

Today we see many girls and boys playing soccer in towns and cities across our country. In fact, the World Cup was even held in the U.S. in 1994. We can thank Pele for helping soccer to become a well-known and popular sport in our country.